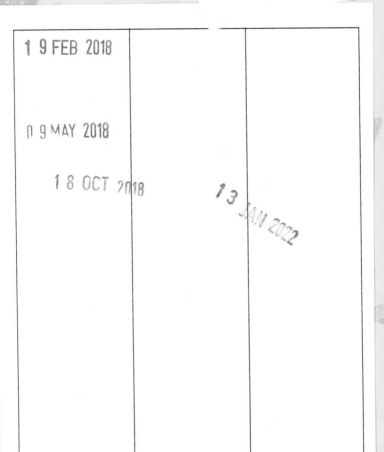

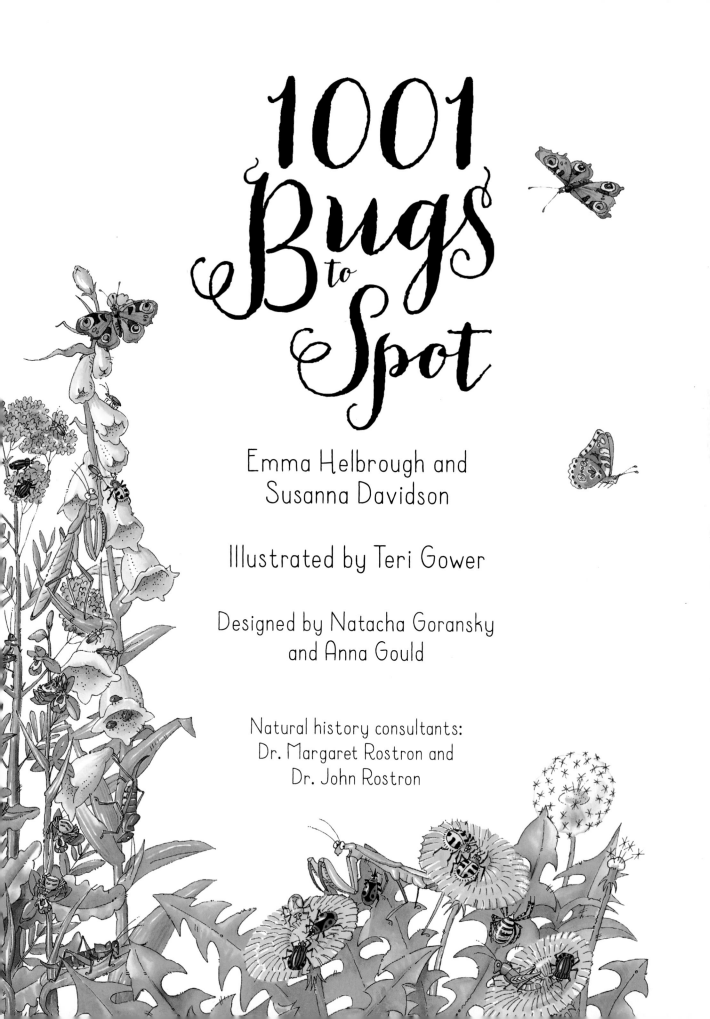

1001 Bugs to Spot

Emma Helbrough and
Susanna Davidson

Illustrated by Teri Gower

Designed by Natacha Goransky
and Anna Gould

Natural history consultants:
Dr. Margaret Rostron and
Dr. John Rostron

Usborne Quicklinks

For links to websites with video clips, activities and amazing facts about bugs, go to the Usborne Quicklinks website at www.usborne.com/quicklinks and enter the keywords '1001 bugs'. Please follow the internet safety guidelines at the Usborne Quicklinks website. We recommend that children are supervised while on the internet.

Contents

How to use this book

The scenes in this book show bugs from around the world. In each scene there are lots of things for you to find and count. There is also a puzzle on pages 34 to 35 with even more bugs to spot. There are 1001 things to spot in this book altogether.

This is a honeybee. Honeybees live all over the world. They collect pollen from flowers and use it to make honey. There is a honeybee flying through every big picture in this book.
Can you spot them all?

4

The number shows you how many
of that thing you need to find.

Jungle floor

In the hot, sticky jungles of Southeast Asia, plants grow thick and fast, providing homes and food for tropical bugs. But not all plants are as harmless as they seem. Some, like the hollow pitcher plant, lure bugs in with their sweet smell and then turn them into bug soup.

7 frog beetles   9 horned spiders   10 pill millipedes   7 harlequin butterflies   2 pink dragonflies

9 yellow stink bugs   8 palm weevils   6 lantern bugs   9 stalk-eyed flies   8 longhorn beetles

The icons show
you what to look
for in each scene.

Look at the world map on pages 6-7
to see where each scene takes place.

Map of the world

There are over 6 million species of bugs, or creepy-crawlies, alive today. This map shows different creepy-crawly habitats around the world.

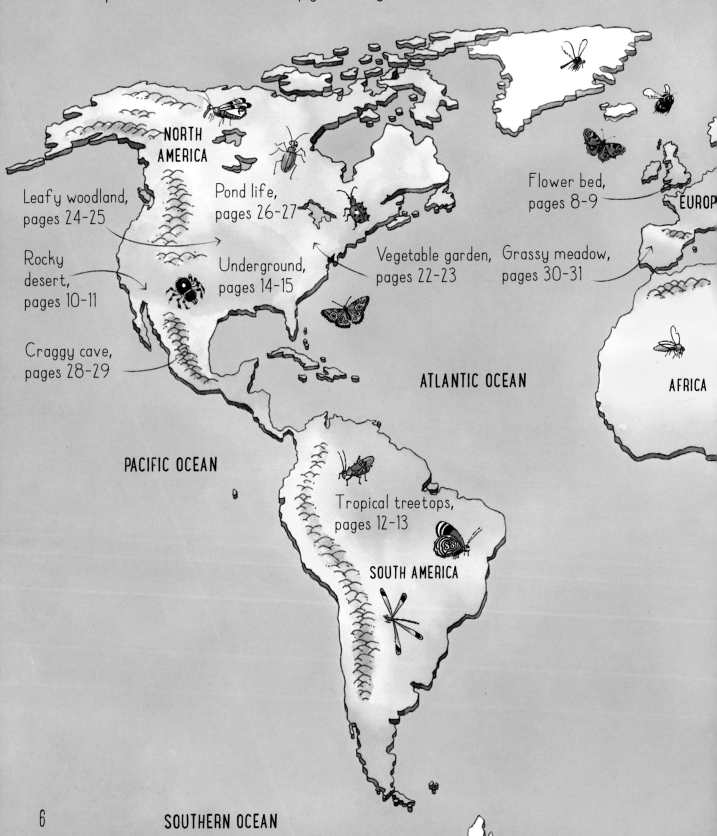

NORTH AMERICA

Leafy woodland, pages 24-25

Pond life, pages 26-27

Flower bed, pages 8-9

EUROP

Rocky desert, pages 10-11

Underground, pages 14-15

Vegetable garden, pages 22-23

Grassy meadow, pages 30-31

Craggy cave, pages 28-29

ATLANTIC OCEAN

AFRICA

PACIFIC OCEAN

Tropical treetops, pages 12-13

SOUTH AMERICA

SOUTHERN OCEAN

ARCTIC OCEAN

ASIA

Garden shed,
pages 18-19

Nightlife,
pages 32-33

Jungle floor,
pages 20-21

PACIFIC OCEAN

INDIAN OCEAN

AUSTRALIA

Sandy desert,
pages 16-17

ANTARCTICA

Flower bed

This flower bed is thick with bugs, all searching for food. Snails munch on the leaves with their rasping tongues, while caterpillars chomp away with their strong jaws. Bees and butterflies flit from flower to flower, drinking nectar with their long tongues.

8

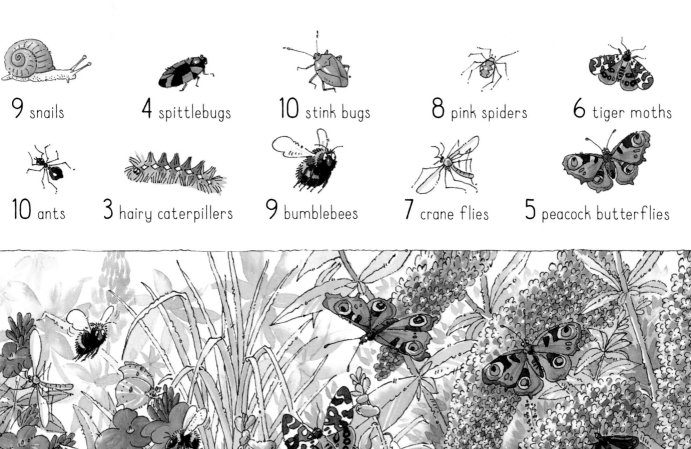

9 snails

4 spittlebugs

10 stink bugs

8 pink spiders

6 tiger moths

10 ants

3 hairy caterpillers

9 bumblebees

7 crane flies

5 peacock butterflies

Rocky desert

The Sonoran Desert, in North America, is home to many different kinds of creepy crawlies. Tarantulas are one of the biggest – grasshoppers, beetles and other spiders need to watch out, as they are all on the tarantula's menu.

10 painted grasshoppers   **4** giant centipedes   **5** curled-up millipedes   **7** queen butterflies

11 hawk wasps   **3** tarantulas   **4** hairy scorpions   **10** ants with seeds   **11** cactus beetles

Tropical treetops

Bugs don't only live on the ground. High in the treetops of
the rainforest, ants and caterpillars roam the branches while
damselflies whir through the air, on the hunt for spiders.

 **9** flag-footed bugs

 10 thorn bugs

 **4** helicopter damselflies

 **1** pink katydid

 9 eighty-eight butterflies

7 horned katydids

6 leaf mantises

8 slug caterpillers

 10 leafcutter ants

2 stick insects

13

Underground

Beneath the surface of the earth, bugs are busy tunnelling and burrowing. Earthworms push themselves through the soil, swallowing earth as they go, while mole crickets use their powerful forelegs to dig deep. Grubs munch on roots, and centipedes hunt for tiny bugs.

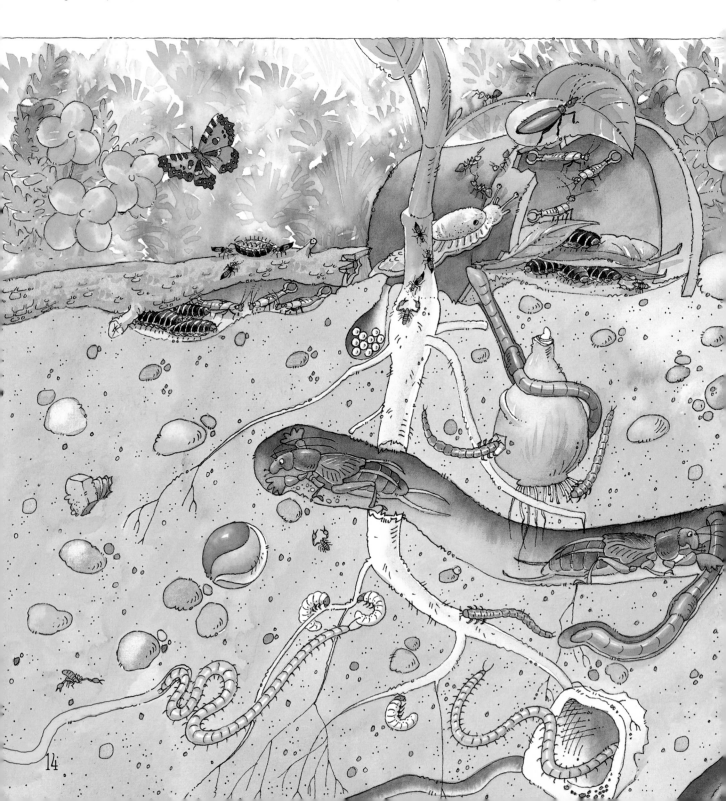

14

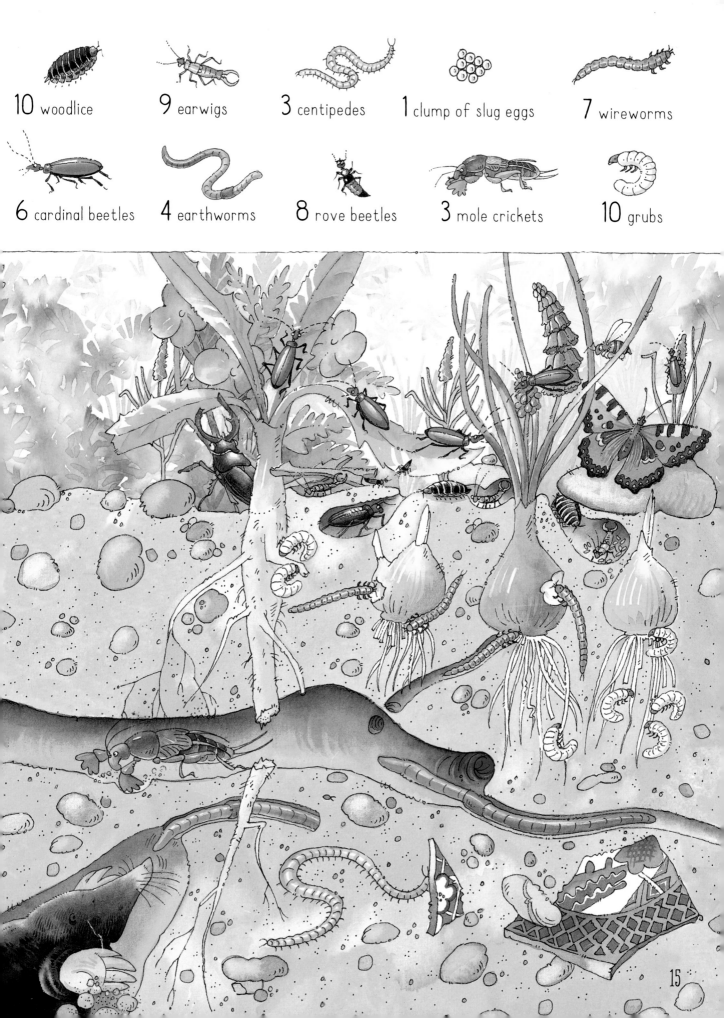

10 woodlice

9 earwigs

3 centipedes

1 clump of slug eggs

7 wireworms

6 cardinal beetles

4 earthworms

8 rove beetles

3 mole crickets

10 grubs

15

Sandy desert

The Namib Desert, in Africa, is the world's oldest desert. It is made up of shifting sand dunes. Thick fog rolls in from the coast, bringing with it enough moisture for many different kinds of bugs to survive.

 5 painted lady butterflies

 8 long-legged beetles

 9 desert crickets

 4 wheel spiders rolling

 10 dune ants

 9 mosquitoes

6 dung beetles

5 sun spiders

 6 thick-tailed scorpions

 10 dune beetles

17

Garden shed

Garden sheds make perfect homes for bugs. They can shelter in cracks and crevices in cold weather, while some creepy-crawlies, such as spiders, will make their homes there all year round.

10 house flies

5 house centipedes

7 woodlouse hunters

8 curled-up woodlice

9 cockroaches

5 spitting spiders

10 fruit flies

7 silverfish

8 wasps

6 house crickets

Jungle floor

In the hot, sticky jungles of Southeast Asia, plants grow thick and fast, providing homes and food for tropical bugs. But not all plants are as harmless as they seem. Some, like the hollow pitcher plant, lure bugs in with their sweet smell and then turn them into bug soup.

7 frog beetles

9 horned spiders

10 pill millipedes

7 harlequin butterflies

2 pink dragonflies

9 yellow stink bugs

8 palm weevils

6 lantern bugs

9 stalk-eyed flies

8 longhorn beetles

21

Vegetable garden

Young and tender plants are irresistable to many bugs. Slugs love to gorge on the leaves, while leafhoppers feed on plant sap with their sucking mouthparts. But lacewings are a gardener's friend, preying on the plant-munching bugs.

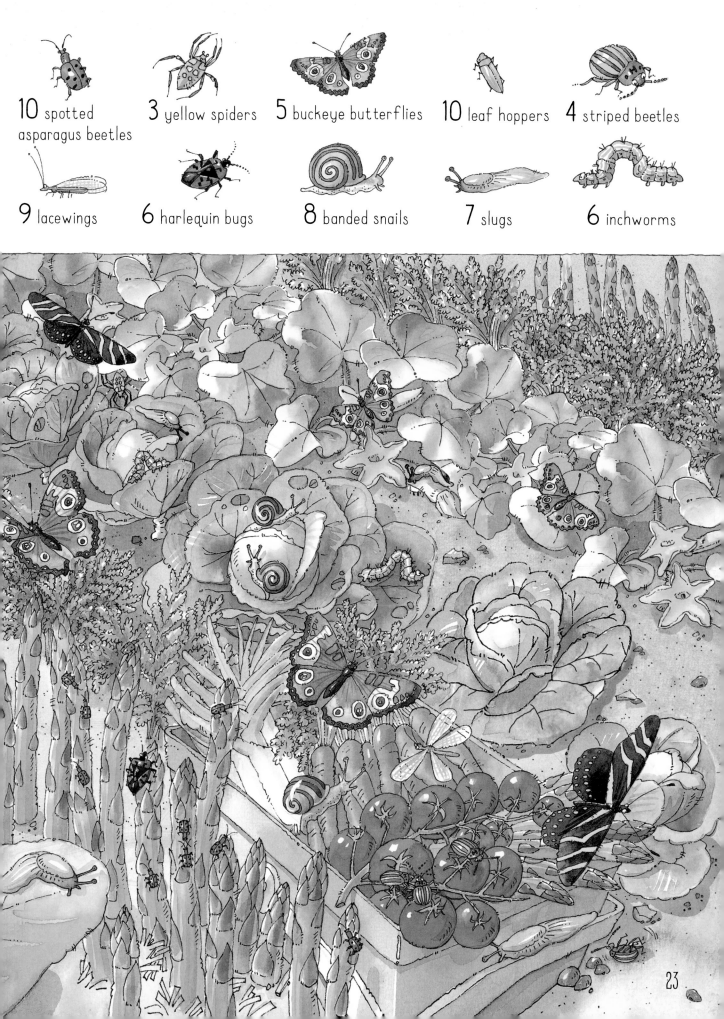

10 spotted asparagus beetles

3 yellow spiders

5 buckeye butterflies

10 leaf hoppers

4 striped beetles

9 lacewings

6 harlequin bugs

8 banded snails

7 slugs

6 inchworms

Leafy woodland

Summer has ended and the woodland floor is covered in a carpet of leaves. Jumping spiders leap across the ground, while banana slugs feast on mushrooms, rotting leaves and plants. Other bugs make their homes beneath tree bark and in pieces of dead wood.

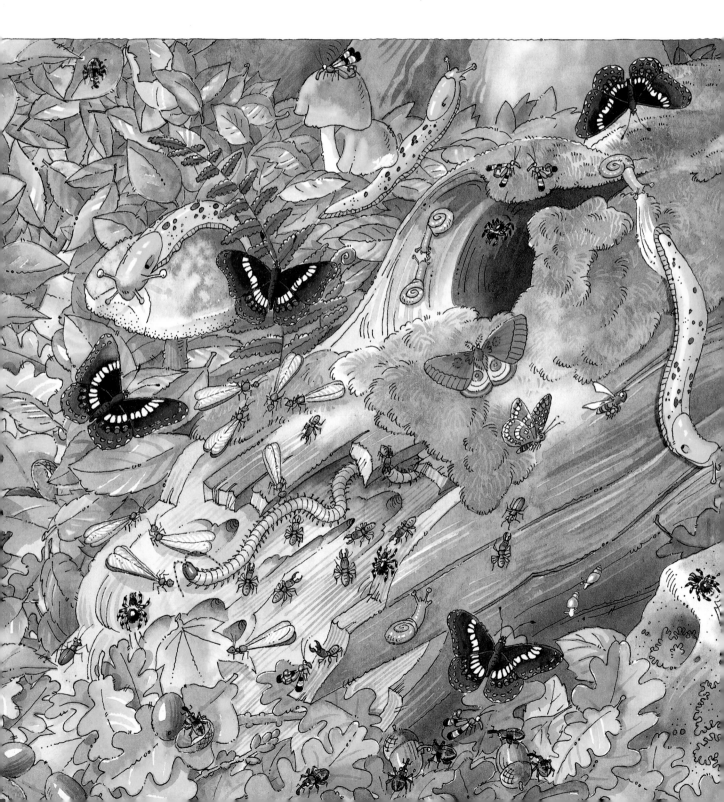

10 soldier termites

9 winged termites

8 acorn weevils

4 banana slugs

8 green tiger beetles

7 scorpion flies

9 fungus beetles

10 jumping spiders

6 io moths

8 flat-disc snails

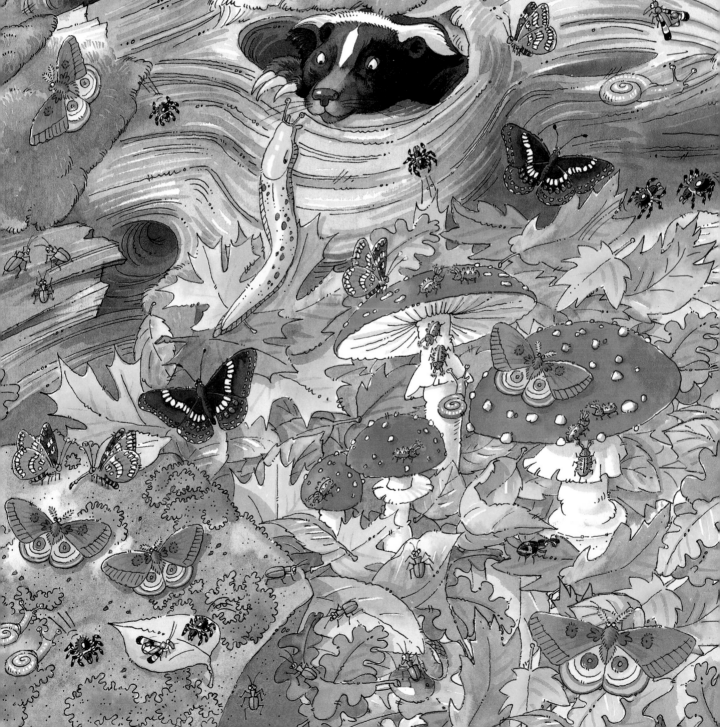

Pond Life

Pond skaters skim across the surface on their feather-light legs, while diving beetles zoom down to the depths on the hunt for prey. On the bottom of the pond, caddisfly larvae make protective cases for themselves out of pebbles and grains of sand.

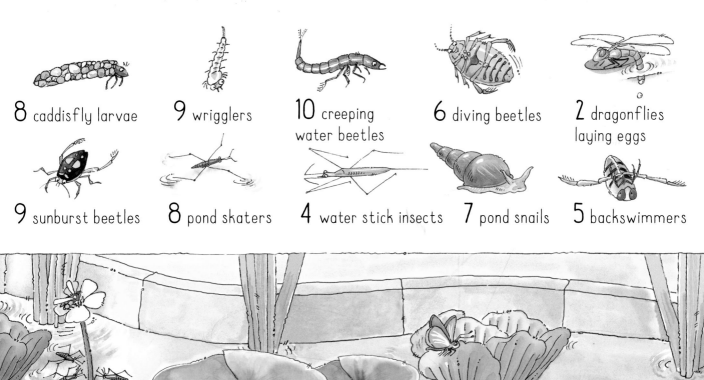

8 caddisfly larvae

9 wrigglers

10 creeping water beetles

6 diving beetles

2 dragonflies laying eggs

9 sunburst beetles

8 pond skaters

4 water stick insects

7 pond snails

5 backswimmers

Craggy cave

This cave is cool, moist and dark. Herald moths hibernate here for up to ten months of the year, while some other bugs, such as cave snails, spend their whole lives inside the cave.

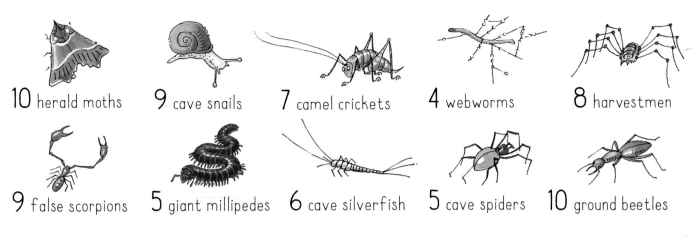

10 herald moths 9 cave snails 7 camel crickets 4 webworms 8 harvestmen

9 false scorpions 5 giant millipedes 6 cave silverfish 5 cave spiders 10 ground beetles

Grassy meadow

The grassy meadows of southern Europe attract butterflies,
flies, wasps and beetles that feed on the pollen and nectar.
These in turn are food for crab spiders and praying mantises,
which snap up their prey in their spiky front legs.

10 fire bugs

9 striped stink bugs

8 bee beetles

5 praying mantises

10 cinnabar caterpillars

7 crab spiders

6 hawk-moth caterpillars

5 wasp spiders

9 bush crickets

7 soldier beetles

Nightlife

It's a hot summer's night. Male cicadas sing to attract females by vibrating their bodies, filling the air with their hum. Fireflies, a type of winged beetle, make their own light, while owlet and inchworm moths are drawn to the lantern's glow.

6 stag beetles

4 cicadas

9 snails with yellow shells

7 blue beetles

3 slant-faced grasshoppers

8 awkling caterpillars

7 inchworm moths

9 fireflies

9 owlet moths

10 weaver ants

More things to spot

At a butterfly house, you can see butterflies from all around the world. Look back through the book and see if you can find and count all these butterflies.

5 comma butterflies

5 swordtails

4 zebra butterflies

6 yellow pansy butterflies

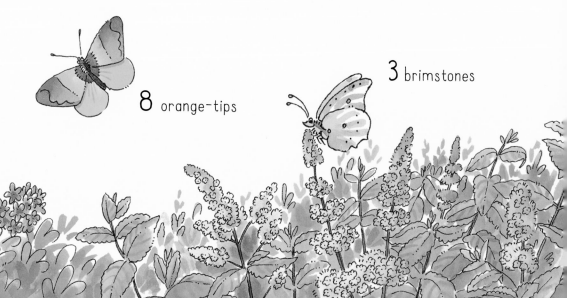

8 orange-tips

3 brimstones

4 fritillaries

4 skipper
butterflies

6 white admirals

2 tortoiseshell butterflies

7 swallowtails

2 blue morpho butterflies

5 sleepy orange
butterflies

5 checkerspots

Habitats

The Earth is made up of lots of different kinds of habitats, from deserts to rainforests. Each bug is perfectly suited to its habitat. Here are some examples:

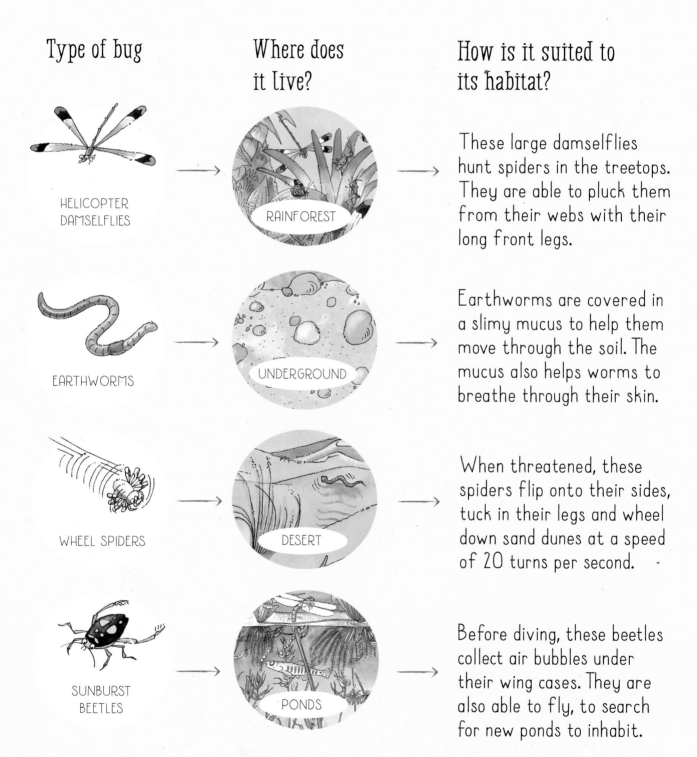

Type of bug	Where does it live?	How is it suited to its habitat?
HELICOPTER DAMSELFLIES	RAINFOREST	These large damselflies hunt spiders in the treetops. They are able to pluck them from their webs with their long front legs.
EARTHWORMS	UNDERGROUND	Earthworms are covered in a slimy mucus to help them move through the soil. The mucus also helps worms to breathe through their skin.
WHEEL SPIDERS	DESERT	When threatened, these spiders flip onto their sides, tuck in their legs and wheel down sand dunes at a speed of 20 turns per second.
SUNBURST BEETLES	PONDS	Before diving, these beetles collect air bubbles under their wing cases. They are also able to fly, to search for new ponds to inhabit.

Web of life

The bugs in a habitat, or ecosystem, depend on each other to survive. Some bugs eat plants, while others hunt and eat other bugs. Food webs show how animals are linked together by what they eat. The arrows point from the prey (what is eaten) to the predators (the creature that eats it).

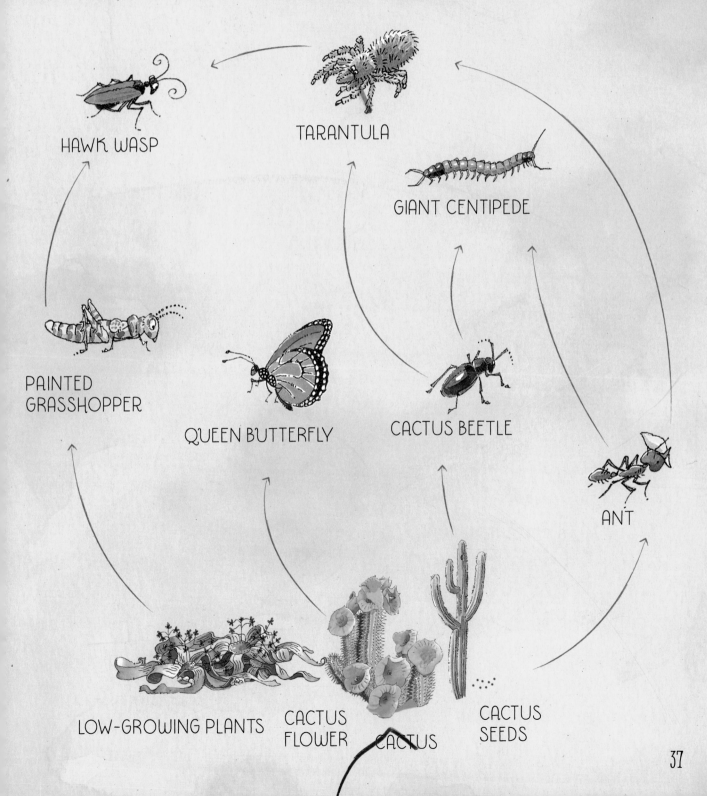

HAWK WASP

TARANTULA

GIANT CENTIPEDE

PAINTED GRASSHOPPER

QUEEN BUTTERFLY

CACTUS BEETLE

ANT

LOW-GROWING PLANTS

CACTUS FLOWER

CACTUS

CACTUS SEEDS

Did you know...?

Here are amazing facts about some of the things to spot in this book.

QUEEN BUTTERFLIES are poisonous to most birds because of the toxins taken in by the caterpillar as it feeds on the milkweed plant.

HAWK WASPS attack spiders, paralyzing them with their sting before dragging them into a den. They then lay an egg inside the spider. When the egg hatches, the larva eats its way out of the still-paralyzed spider.

LEAFCUTTER ANTS grow their own food in underground fungus farms. They carry pieces of leaves, up to 50 times their own body weight, which are used to create fungus to feed the colony.

DUNG BEETLES get their name from their diet: they eat other animals' dung. Some species roll the dung into balls for females to lay their eggs in (known as brood balls) or for adults to feed on.

FRUIT FLIES can reproduce incredibly quickly. Females lay hundreds of eggs which hatch into maggots within 30 hours. The maggots become fruit flies in a couple of weeks and are then able to reproduce themselves.

STRIPED STINK BUGS have bright markings to warn predators that they taste disgusting.

STAG BEETLES are one of Europe's largest ground-dwelling insects. The males have huge antler-like jaws, which are used for wrestling rival males rather than biting.

LANTERN BUGS have long, hollow 'snouts' which they use as straws to suck up sap from trees. Despite their name, they don't actually glow in the dark.

SOLDIER TERMITES live in large groups, called colonies. Their job is to defend their colony from attack and protect the worker termites that forage for food.

Answers

Did you find all the butterflies in the book? Here's where they are:

5 comma butterflies: Flower bed (pages 8-9)

4 zebra butterflies: Vegetable garden (pages 22-23)

8 orange-tips: Grassy meadow (pages 30-31)

5 swordtails: Jungle floor (pages 20-21)

6 yellow pansy butterflies: Sandy desert (pages 16-17)

3 brimstones: Flower bed (pages 8-9)

4 fritillaries: Garden shed (pages 18-19)

6 white admirals: Leafy woodland (pages 24-25)

7 swallowtails: Grassy meadow (pages 30-31)

5 sleepy orange butterflies: Rocky desert (pages 10-11)

4 skipper butterflies: Pond life (pages 26-27)

2 tortoiseshell butterflies: Underground (pages 14-15)

2 blue morpho butterflies: Tropical treetops (pages 12-13)

5 checkerspots: Leafy woodland (pages 24-25)

Index

Digital artworking and retouching by Mike Olley and John Russell

Edited by Anna Milbourne and Jane Chisholm

The publishers would like to thank Carl Cantaluppi, Horticulture Agent at North Carolina State University and Dr. Gordon Wardell, Presient of the S.A.F.E. Research and Development, for their helpful advice.

My Very First Book of

PIRATES

retold by Richard Walker
illustrated by Olwyn Whelan

Barefoot Books
Celebrating Art and Story

for Rowena and Kate – R.W.

for my mother and father,
and for Michael – O.W.

CONTENTS

The Captain's Goose

SCANDINAVIAN

Long, long ago, in a distant land, there lived a great sea captain. He was stronger and braver than any sea captain who lived before or after him. He was a sworn enemy of all pirates. It takes a lot to scare a brave pirate, but this sea captain was so mighty in battle that all evildoers kept well away from him. He had a reputation for honesty and everybody wanted him for a friend.

One evening, the captain was sitting in his cabin waiting for his cook to bring him a goose which had been roasted for his dinner. He could smell the appetising fragrance wafting in from the kitchen and his mouth was watering. He had had a busy day and he was looking forward to the delicious meal the cook was preparing for him.

Suddenly, the cabin door opened and in walked a wizard. The wizard was dressed in a long robe with a staff in his hand.

'Greetings, Captain,' he said. 'I have heard of your courage and honesty. I know of your strength. I am here to ask whether being a mere sea captain is enough for you, or whether you would prefer to be a king?'

The sea captain was rather taken aback by the wizard's question, but it

didn't take him long to gather his wits and give his answer. He was so good at keeping order that for months now all the pirates, and with them any hint of trouble, kept well out of his way. To be honest, he was really rather fed up with his life. Apart from the occasional storm, nothing exciting had happened to him in a long time.

'It would be a new challenge to be a king,' he said, 'but how could it be so?'

'For me, everything is possible,' said the wizard. 'I can easily arrange for you to be a king. All I would ask in return is that you give me ten golden coins each year in gratitude.'

'It would be worth more than that,' said the captain.

'Yet that is still all I ask,' said the wizard. 'Now, if you really want to be a king, you must come with me.'

So the captain forgot all about his dinner and followed the wizard. As soon as they were out of the cabin, the wizard touched the captain with his staff to make him invisible, so that none of the crew could see what was happening. Then the wizard uttered a strange spell and a magical boat appeared out of nowhere. Together, the wizard and the captain travelled in his boat far across the sea to a land where the king had just died. It was a very beautiful land, with high mountains and deep fjords. The mountains were full of gold mines and the fjords were full of fish, so many people wanted to control it. But the dead king had only one son and heir, a child who was just ten years old. Word had already got around to the pirates and their boats were crowded into the little harbour. They knew they could easily deal with a child and that the country could soon be their pirate kingdom.

The royal advisors didn't know what to do and were having a meeting in the great chamber when the wizard and the sea captain walked in.

'Gentlemen, you are in a difficult position,' said the wizard to them. 'The boy is too young to be king and to fight the pirates. You need a strong leader if you want to maintain order.'

'We know – but what else can we do?'

'Listen to me,' replied the wizard. 'I have here a man truly fit to be king. He could chase away the pirates without any trouble at all. Why not choose him instead of the lad?'

'Can we do that?' The royal advisors looked hopefully at the captain.

'If you don't, there will be no kingdom for anyone to rule,' said the captain. 'Let me go to the harbour and face the pirates alone. If I can get rid of them by myself then make me your king ... if not, then let the boy try.'

This was quickly agreed and the sea captain walked boldly down to the harbour. You can imagine the commotion when the pirates saw their old enemy striding across the cobblestones towards their boats. They had all fought him before and he had always beaten them, no matter what they had tried or how many men they had had on their side.

'There's nothing for us here,' said a big, black-bearded pirate, 'not if the captain is going to be king. Come on lads, let's find our pickings somewhere else.'

Soon the little harbour was empty of ships flying the skull and crossbones. Not long afterwards, the sea captain was crowned king with great pomp and ceremony. To tell the truth, he was a fine king. He was honest and fair and everyone was happy. The first year of his reign soon went by. When the wizard came for his first payment, the king was glad to give him the ten golden coins.

Another good year passed and the wizard came again. Once more, the sea captain gave him the payment he had been promised. But now the royal advisors began to mutter about it and before the third year had passed, they went to the king.

'Why should our money go to this wizard,' they said, 'when all he did was to bring you here? After all, you were the one who got rid of the pirates.'

The king thought long and hard about this and found he agreed with them.

He forgot that, without the wizard's help, he would never have found his way to this beautiful land. So the next time the wizard came to get his payment, the king refused to give it to him.

'I did all the work,' said the king. 'All you did was to bring me here. For that favour you've had two payments of ten golden coins, which is more than enough. Now, away with you, before I send for the guards!'

The moment the king said these words, the wizard's eyes blazed. 'So be it!' he declared, raising his magic staff. At once, there was a bright flash, the castle and all the royal advisors vanished and the next thing he knew the sea captain was back in his cabin. The door opened and in walked his cook with the succulent roast goose. Once again, he was just a sea captain – and that is why we sometimes say of somebody: 'His goose is cooked.' For when your goose is cooked, there is always a lesson to be learnt.

Robin Hood and the Pirates

ENGLISH

It was a hot, summer day in Sherwood Forest. Even the canopy of leaves on top of the trees couldn't keep the heat out and there wasn't a whisper of a breeze. As if that wasn't bad enough, everybody seemed to have gone away – even the Sheriff of Nottingham. For the outlaws, there was nobody to rob and no fun to be had. Life was very dull indeed.

Robin Hood and his Merry Men were lazing around when suddenly Robin stood up and said, 'I've had enough of this. There's nothing to do. I've got to get away for a while and have a holiday. I think I'll go to the seaside.'

'I've heard that Scarborough is nice,' said Little John, 'but it's a long journey.'

'That's all right,' said Robin, 'I've got a good horse. I'll set off tomorrow and you can be in charge until I get back.'

The next day, Robin set out bright and early. It was still hot but at least he was doing something. The journey to Scarborough took a couple of days but he enjoyed seeing new places on the way. It seemed no time at all before he crossed the Yorkshire moors and reached Scarborough. From the top of the town, he saw the little harbour nestling around the castle on its rock.

He left his horse grazing in a field and walked into town, carrying his bow and quiver of arrows on his shoulder.

He had not gone far before people started to stop and stare at him.

'Hello, stranger,' said one of them, 'and what would you be doing in these parts?'

'Just taking a holiday,' said Robin. 'I need somewhere to stay.'

'You could try the widow Bates, she's usually got a spare room and the money will be useful to her.

It's just down the street on your left. The house with the black door.'

Robin thanked him and found his way to the house.

'Yes, I've room enough,' said the widow. 'What's your name?'

Robin wasn't sure whether they would have heard of him and, in any case, he was on holiday. He decided it would be better not to tell her who he was.

'My name is Simon Wise,' he said.

'I'll call you Simon, then, and you can call me Martha.'

For a few days Robin had a great time in Scarborough. He roamed around the streets, walked on the beach and watched the fishing boats coming in and out of the harbour. It was certainly quite different to life in Sherwood Forest. But before long he grew restless. At breakfast one morning, he told the widow that he was bored.

'I own a fishing boat,' said the widow. 'You can always go and crew with the fishermen if you want something to do.'

'I think I might give that a try,' said Robin. He had never been on a boat before and he was ready for an adventure. Early the next morning he joined the crew down at the harbour.

'Sit there,' ordered one of the men. Robin quietly took his place on the little boat as it left the harbour bobbing up and down on the waves.

17

The men didn't say much and, to tell the truth, weren't all that happy to have a stranger with them. Silently, they dropped mackerel lines over the edge of the boat and soon they were pulling up shiny mackerel by the score. But nobody bothered to give Robin a line. All he could do was sit and watch as the others exchanged jokes and baited their hooks. When the fishermen got back to shore that evening, there was no share of the catch for him, just the laughter of the men as he walked away.

To their surprise, Robin was down at the harbour again the next morning, but this time he took his bow and arrows with him.

'Well, Simon Wise,' said the captain, 'you weren't very "wise" yesterday because you didn't bring a mackerel line with you. Today you're even less "wise" if you think you can catch fish with an arrow.'

'We'll see,' said Robin quietly as he climbed on board.

The fishermen had not been out at sea for long when there was panic
among the crew as they saw a sailing ship bearing down on them.

'It's French pirates!' cried the captain. 'We had better go below deck and
hope they leave us alone.'

'What are you afraid of?' asked Robin. 'You can go below if you want, but
first tie me to the mast and give me my bow and arrows.'

Everyone thought he had gone mad but they did as he said and then went
below leaving him alone. Tied firmly to the mast, Robin moved up and down
with the waves. This made it difficult to aim, but at least he was able to draw
his bow without losing his balance. As soon as the pirates came into range he
let fly with the first arrow and shot one of them. The second and third arrows
also hit their marks. Soon the pirate captain appeared on deck and shouted,
'Peace! We surrender!'

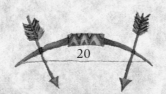

Then Robin called to the fishermen to come up on deck. Somehow they managed to get their boat alongside the pirate ship and board it. At Robin's command, they tied up all of the pirates. Then they triumphantly sailed the vessel back into the harbour. Of course, everybody came to meet them. The pirate hold was full of gold and silver and precious gems and everyone helped to unload it. Then they freed the captain, gave him back his boat and warned him never to sail close to Scarborough again. The pirate captain fled, relieved that he and his men had escaped without losing their lives. There was singing and dancing in Scarborough that night and a great feast was held in honour of their hero, Simon Wise.

Robin insisted on sharing the treasure with the crew of the fishing boat, who now agreed that Simon was very 'wise' after all. They were delighted to have become rich men overnight, but Robin had had enough of holidaying and wanted to get back to his Merry Men. The last thing he wanted was to have to carry a lot of money with him because he didn't want to tempt any outlaws along the way. Instead, he gave his share to the widow and she in turn used some of it to pay for a hospital to be built. Robin went home to Sherwood Forest and told his Merry Men about his fishing adventure. But he never returned to Scarborough. Instead, the next time he had a holiday, he went a little further up the coast, to a place which is called 'Robin Hood's Bay' to this very day.

The Kobold and the Pirates

GERMAN

Jake was a cabin-boy, which was just what he wanted to be. He loved the smell of the sea, he loved the sound of the wind in the rigging and the creaking of the ship as it rolled with the waves. He knew that this was the life for him. Jake should have been happy, but he wasn't. For though he loved the ocean waves, he worked for a captain who treated him very badly. And there was worse than that – the ship was a pirate ship.

One day, Jake was setting the table for dinner when the captain growled, 'What's the use of having a fool of a boy like you? You never do anything right. How many places have you set?'

'Why, just one, sir ... isn't that right?' Jake trembled as he answered.

'Of course not!' yelled the captain. 'Tonight I dine with Klabauterman. Set a place for him and make sure there's plenty of food and wine. Get a move on, boy, or I'll have you flogged!'

Jake quietly did as he was told and then stood aside to await the guest. He had the surprise of his life when the captain sat down opposite the empty place and started to talk.

24

'I must say we're having fair weather and a good voyage. It keeps the crew happy and they're not such a bad lot. What do you think of them, eh?'

Jake was confused. One minute the captain was furious with him and the next he was chatting away as if they were friends.

'Oh, the crew are fine, sir,' he said. 'I'm pleased to be one of them.'

'What!' roared the captain. 'Who told you to speak? I'm not talking to you, young lad. I'm talking to my guest! Get out of here!'

Jake didn't need telling twice. He ran out of the cabin on to the deck and stood there, catching his breath. Then he heard two voices coming from the captain's cabin. One was the captain's, but he had never heard the other voice before.

'I'm sorry,' spluttered Jake, 'but I don't understand what's happening. The captain made me lay another place but nobody sat at it, then the captain talked to it and now it's answering him ... but it's empty. Are we haunted? What's going on?'

'Steady, lad,' said the cook with a kindly smile. 'It's nothing for you to worry about. The captain's dining with Klabauterman, that's all.'

'But who is Klabauterman?'

'I like that young lad,' the voice said. 'True, he could be better dressed and he's barefoot, but he looks honest. Look after him. Treat him well.'

'What, that cabin boy?' spluttered the captain. 'You want me to look after him?'

'That's what I said.'

It was all too much for Jake and he rushed to the galley where the cook was busy making the crew's supper. Jake ran head first into his fat, round stomach.

'Careful!' puffed the cook. 'What's the rush?'

'He's the kobold of the sea.' Jake looked even more confused, so the cook stopped what he was doing and sat down to explain. 'Back home, a lot of places have kobolds. They're the spirits that look after things. They live in houses, down mines, in all sorts of places. If you have one living with you it will bring you good luck. The sea kobold is very powerful. If he wants he can make storms and gales, hurricanes and whirlpools. Above all though, he loves food and if his stomach is full of good things he stays happy and calm. I'm pleased to say that he likes my cooking and this is the third voyage we've had him with us. Usually he dines with me in the galley but tonight he's dining with the captain.'

'But why can't I see him?'

'It would be bad news for you if you did,' the cook replied. 'You only see him when you're about to die. They say he's dressed all in yellow with bright red hair, but I'd rather not find out for myself.'

From then on, life on board was not so bad for Jake. He still had to do all the nasty jobs and the captain still treated him just as badly. Somehow though, he felt he had a friend. He could often feel the kobold near him. And he could sense that the kobold wasn't happy with the way Jake was being treated.

One day, the pirate ship sailed into a thick sea mist. It was very difficult to see, but after a while the captain announced that he could see another ship coming towards them.

'It looks like a merchant ship to me,' he shouted. 'All hands on deck! Load the cannon, hoist the black flag! Look lively, lads, there's booty to be had!'

In all the commotion Jake heard the kobold.

'Not this one, it's a phantom ship!'

But nobody took any notice.

'Well, I did my best,' the spirit said. 'Don't you worry though, Jake. Get some food and water together and take one of the small boats. It's time we found you another captain.'

Jake did as he was told. Nobody noticed him as the phantom ship bore down on the pirates.

'Fire!' shouted the captain. The gun roared and the cannonball shot straight at the other ship but it passed right through and out the other side. Still the strange ship came towards them. 'Again, lads, fire again!'

It was too late. The ship was almost upon them. Then the captain saw, sitting on the bowsprit, a little man dressed all in yellow with flaming red hair.

'It's the kobold!'

31

But none of the others could see anything. They were too busy abandoning ship as the phantom vessel ploughed on, cutting their boat in two.

Alone in his boat, Jake rowed for all he was worth. Soon the mist cleared and he saw another ship in full sail.

'Ahoy there,' he shouted. 'For pity's sake, save me!'

I'm pleased to say that the crew did just that. Soon Jake was warm and dry in a cabin. Sitting opposite him was another captain, but one who smiled a friendly smile as his cabin boys set the table for a meal.

'Shall I just lay two places, sir?'

'No,' the captain said kindly, 'make it three if you would. I think the kobold will be joining us.'

Pirate Grace

IRISH

Grace O'Malley was no ordinary pirate; she was a member of the O'Malley family, a powerful Irish clan who owned several castles and a mighty fleet of merchant ships. Grace liked nothing better than to be out on the high seas, and when she set sail, everyone on the west coast of Ireland recognised her, for she was famous across land and sea.

One spring evening, Grace was a long way from home when she began to feel particularly tired and hungry. She and her men were on their way back from a long trading expedition; the ship's supply of food had run low and the crew were soaked to the skin by heavy rain. Grace needed a break and a meal. So when she saw the lights of Howth glittering in the distance, she ordered her helmsman to sail into the harbour; the castle there would be as good a place as any for her and her men to stop awhile.

Now in those days, it was the custom for all Gaelic chieftains to offer hospitality to any member of another friendly clan who was passing through their territory. But when Grace and her men approached the castle gates, they were surprised to find them locked and barred.

'Is anyone at home?' Grace bellowed, and she rattled on the gates until a servant came running up.

'Who is it?' called a timid voice from the other side of the gate.

'It's Grace O'Malley come to visit his lordship. Go and tell your master he has some visitors. We're wet and hungry and we need a decent meal. Be quick about it, now!'

The servant did not need to be asked twice. He had never met Grace, but he knew that it would not be wise to fall out with her. So he hurried away through the corridors of the castle to announce her arrival.

In the dining room, the lord of Howth was about to start his evening meal. The table was groaning with succulent meats.

'Excuse me, my lord, Grace O'Malley is at the door. She wants to come in and dine with you. Shall I bring her to you?'

But his master's face darkened. 'Certainly not!' he roared. 'Can't you see I'm eating? Tell her I'm too busy to be disturbed. Besides, it's almost night-time. She'll have to go away.'

'But ...'

The poor servant scuttled nervously back to the front door. He knew how dangerous Grace could be. He had even heard a rumour that she slept with a rope that led from her favourite ship to her big toe. In the event of any trouble, a pull on the rope would bring her running. So he stood well back from the gates and called out:

'I'm sorry, Mistress Grace. My master says that he is too busy to see you. Can you come another time perhaps?'

'Another time? Doesn't he know that it's pouring with rain? What's he doing that's so important? Has he forgotten the rule of hospitality?'

'But what?'

'But surely we should do something for her. After all, isn't she the most famous pirate in the land? It wouldn't do to fall out with her; it wouldn't do at all.'

'Do you think I'm frightened by the likes of Grace O'Malley? Humph! Tell her to clear off and stop standing there shaking in your socks! Now, let me enjoy my meal in peace.'

With that, the lord picked up his knife and started to carve a juicy side of beef for himself.

Even with the gate between them, the servant was so scared that he
blurted out the truth:

'He's in the middle of his dinner, Miss. He says he wants to enjoy it
in peace and quiet.'

'He's having a meal!' Grace roared back. 'And he won't share it!
Well, he may live to regret it!'

Then she spun round on her heels and led her crew back down to the
harbour. Through the half-light, she could see a young boy dragging
his boat on to the beach, alongside her own. Grace stopped in her
tracks.

'Who are you?' she demanded.

'I live here,' the boy answered simply. 'This is my father's castle. Who
are you?'

Without stopping to explain, Grace seized the lad and dragged him
on to her boat. The boy kicked and screamed and tried to bite, but she
was more than a match for him. She used an old rope to bind his arms
and legs, and a kerchief to gag him. Now she had a hostage that
would bring the lord of Howth to his senses! Swiftly and silently,
Grace and her men sailed out of the harbour. They kept sailing right
through the night until they came to Clare Island Castle, the
O'Malleys' stronghold.

Back at Howth, no one could understand what had happened to the lord's heir; but the servant who had answered the gate to Grace had his suspicions. Search parties were sent out up and down the coast, but although the boy's rowing boat was found safely moored, there was no sign of the child. The lord of Howth was beside himself with fear. What had happened to his beloved son? Had he been drowned, kidnapped or murdered?

He did not have to wait long to find out. After a few days, a message was delivered to the castle. 'If you wish to see your son alive,' it read, 'Grace O'Malley invites you to visit him at her home on Clare Island.'

Now the lord of Howth regretted his folly, for the waters around Clare Island were known to be treacherous and many sailors had lost their lives on the rocks there. Before he embarked, he found a local fisherman to act as his guide. The fisherman's boat bobbed like a cork on the waves: the lord of Howth turned green and then he turned grey. At last, the fisherman steered the boat safely into the bay. A servant greeted them and led them in solemn silence to meet Grace.

The lord of Howth entered with as much dignity as he could muster. He was sick as a dog and his legs were nearly collapsing beneath him, but he looked Grace O'Malley straight in the eye:

'Forgive me for sending you away,' he said. 'Name your price and whatever it is, I shall pay it. Only let me take my dear son home with me!'

Grace looked back at him. She was still smarting with fury, but she felt sorry for the man, and for his child. She smiled quietly, holding his gaze.

'I don't want your money, or your son,' she replied slowly. 'Instead, I demand an apology ...'

'You have it, you have it!'

'... and not just an apology, but a vow.'

'Yes?'

'From this day on, the doors of your castle must never be barred to anyone looking for shelter. Not only that ... in future, you must always lay a spare place at your dining table in case anyone should need it.'

Then the lord of Howth bowed his head and made the vow. His son was returned to him, safe and well, and Grace even offered him a meal before they left.

Maybe the lord of Howth had got away with his foolishness lightly, but he honoured his promise and so, in his turn, did his son. In fact, I am told that even to this day, there is always a spare place at the dinner table of his castle.

Music Charms the Pirates

JAPANESE

Long ago in Japan, there was a boy called Mochimitsu. He loved music and spent all his spare time practising. People marvelled at his playing but to be honest, some of them thought it was a bit of a waste of time.

'He'd be better off studying. Why doesn't he help around the house? He's just lazy.'

That was the view of the grown-ups. As for children of his own age, they couldn't understand why he wasn't out having fun with them.

'Come and play,' they would say to him, 'we're playing pirates today and it will be fun. Come on ... music will never help you in a fight!'

But Mochimitsu just carried on practising and learning more and more tunes. He even began to write some of his own.

Time went by and Mochimitsu grew up to become a famous musician. He travelled and played all over Japan and people paid to hear him. They filled the halls wherever he went. Soon he became very rich and even had his own boat which he loved almost as much as his music.

One day, Mochimitsu was on his way home from a visit to Tottori province.

42

The weather was delightful and the sea gentle and calm. Mochimitsu just let the boat drift along as he sat in the sun on his cabin roof composing a new piece of music.

'Life is so good,' he thought to himself. But suddenly, he began to feel uneasy. When he looked up, he saw a large junk bearing down on him. As it came closer he could see that it was full of some of the most wicked looking people he'd ever seen. And when he saw their guns and swords waving in the air, he knew that he was about to be attacked by pirates. Soon the pirates were swarming over the side of his little ship and clustering around his cabin trying to reach him on the roof. He looked down at a sea of cruel and vicious faces and had to dodge away from the swords that were being thrust at him.

'I'm not armed!' he shouted. 'Take whatever you want. Just leave me alone.'

'What we want is your ship,' said the pirate chief, 'but we don't want you on it. You don't look strong enough to be a slave. I don't think you're rich enough to hold for ransom. Maybe we'll just string you up.'

There was a roar of approval from the other pirates.

Mochimitsu had to think fast.

'I know there's nothing I can do to stop you,' he said. 'It looks as though you're going to kill me. But please can I have one last request before I die?'

'What's that?' roared one of the pirates.

'I am a musician and I live for my music. When I saw you I had just finished a new tune, possibly the best I have ever written. Can I please play it just once before you finish me off?'

The pirate chief thought about this for a while. He was in no hurry and there was no way his prisoner could escape. Maybe it would be good to hear a few tunes.

'Why not?' he said. 'Settle down, lads – we're going to hear some music!'

Some of the pirates laughed scornfully at the musician, but they did as they were told and sat on the deck as Mochimitsu began to play. It was as though he put his whole being into the music. He played better than he ever played before and the beautiful sound drifted over the ocean. It seemed to fill the whole world and even the cruellest of the pirates could not help being moved by it. The music filled their hard hearts. Tears filled their eyes and then began to run down their grubby, evil faces.

45

The pirates listened in silence until the tune ended and the music was no more. Even then they still sat quietly, as the magic of it still held them. It was a while before the captain spoke.

'I know that we are hard men, but maybe life has made us that way. Each one of us started as a child with people who loved us and your playing has brought back memories of those times. We like easy money and adventure too much for us to change, but there is one thing I know. None of us could possibly harm you now. We came to rob you and take your ship, to kill you if need be, but go in peace.'

Slowly and quietly, the band of villains stood up and went back to their pirate junk. Slowly and quietly, they sailed away leaving Mochimitsu playing softly to himself on his cabin roof. As he did so, he thought back to when he was a boy and his friends had said to him, 'Music will never help you in a fight!'

'How wrong you were,' he said to himself, '...well, this time at least!'

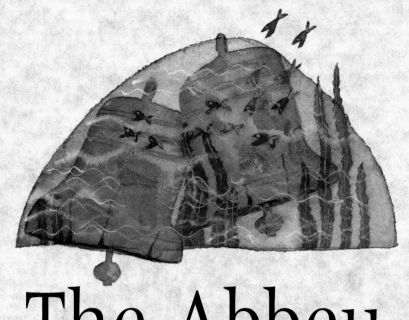

The Abbey
Bells

SCOTTISH

There was once an abbey in Scotland where the monks worked hard for the glory of God. They had many valuable objects to look after – golden candlesticks, a crucifix studded with precious stones, pictures by famous artists, special cups, giant tapestries and wonderful robes. But all the monks agreed that their most precious treasure was the abbey bells. For in the bell tower they had a peal of bells that made the most glorious sound you could ever imagine. The monks took good care of all their treasures, but more than anything, they loved to hear the bells.

All of the monks were happy fellows but Brother John was the happiest. Strong and keen, he was new to the abbey and loved to ring the bells. Each day he would be up in the tower pulling on the bell ropes and watching the bells swinging to and fro above his head. But it was the sound that he really loved. It seemed to reach to heaven itself. The only thing he liked almost as much as the bells was sleeping and it took a lot of effort to wake him up.

The abbey was quite remote but it was close to the sea. Each night the monks would go to sleep to the sound of lapping waves. Sometimes they

would see ships and occasionally someone would row ashore to visit them. That way they kept up to date with what was happening in the world outside. When pirates were in the area putting ashore to rob and plunder from the lonely crofts and houses, the monks were always among the first to hear about it.

One summer morning, the monks were visited by a local farmer. 'There are pirates about, my good brothers,' the farmer warned. 'Whatever you do, don't make too much noise. You would be in trouble if the pirates got to hear about you and all the precious things you have here.'

The monks agreed to keep a look-out. They found a cave nearby where they could hide themselves and their treasure should they ever need to. That was all they did though, and life went on much as it always had.

Early one morning, the monk who was on look-out duty at the abbey saw a strange boat which had dropped anchor in the nearby bay. He could just make out a black flag fluttering from the mast ... it was pirates, and he could see them readying their rowing boats to come ashore.

Not daring to make a commotion in case the pirates heard, the monk ran among the brothers and quietly told them what he had seen.

'Don't make any fuss,' whispered the Abbot, 'but I think we had better get ourselves and our treasure hidden. All together now – but be quiet about it.'

The monks picked up their precious things and left in a procession by the back door. All of the monks but one. Brother John didn't leave with them because he was still asleep. He slept and he snored until even he had slept enough and then he yawned, rubbed his bleary eyes and sat up.

'Goodness,' he thought as he looked around the empty dormitory, 'they must have let me have a lie-in, I wonder why? Still, I'm awake now ... time to ring the bells.'

He stumbled sleepily across to the bell tower, opened the door and gazed lovingly at the bell ropes.

Meanwhile the pirates had rowed ashore armed to the teeth to find out if there was anything to steal. The abbey was quite well hidden and they had missed it as they scouted round. 'This is a waste of time, let's get back,' the bo'son said.

Then the bells started to ring. 'Aha,' said the bo'son, 'let's find out where those bells are!'

Brother John was enjoying himself as he swung on the ropes, but he stopped short when the door flew open and all the pirates burst in. What an evil looking bunch they were! They tied him up and then barged all around the place looking for treasure, but the abbey was deserted and there was nothing to interest them.

'The only valuable things they've got are the bells,' the pirate captain muttered angrily. 'At least we can take the bells! Look lively, you lot. Get them aboard and let's be on our way!'

It was hard work taking down the bells and carrying them to the shore. It was even harder work rowing them across to the pirate ship but at last they managed it and got them stashed below decks. The pirates even forgot about Brother John who was powerless to prevent his beloved bells from being

taken away. Once the pirates had gone, the other monks came out of hiding and found him all alone in the bell tower.

'The pirates have stolen our bells,' cried John. 'What are we going to do?'

'Never mind,' said the Abbot. 'They'll do those pirates no good either on land or on water. We can always get some more bells.'

The Abbot was right. As soon as the pirates hoisted the sails and weighed anchor the bells started rolling about in the hold. They rolled with the pitching of the sea and as they did so they rang out as if they were laughing at the pirates. Then, one by one, they crashed through the side of the ship and sank beneath the waves. Water poured in through the holes they had made and the wicked pirates had to lower their rowing boats into the waves and row for their lives.

Back at the abbey the first thing the Abbot did was to order a new set of bells. When they arrived Brother John was the first monk to be allowed to ring them. As for the old bells, they settled down on the bed of the ocean and to this day, as the currents flow around them, there are times when you can still hear their watery chimes.

The Ship
of Bones

MOROCCAN

Long ago and far away a rich merchant and his servant took passage on a small sailing ship bound for Tangiers. All went well until a storm blew up and fierce waves battered their fragile little craft. The crew battled valiantly but finally their ship sank. Cold, wet and frightened, the survivors clasped bits of floating wreckage as the storm raged around them. The merchant and his servant gripped tightly on to a piece of wood which was hurled about on the furious sea.

Just as quickly as it had arrived, the storm blew away, leaving the two men exhausted and alone. They drifted through the night and into the next day. With no food to eat or fresh water to drink they began to think the end was near. Then they saw a strange-looking ship sailing close to them.

'We're saved,' the merchant gasped. 'Shout for help. Make sure they see us.'

They yelled for all they were worth, but the ship just sailed on.

'We have to reach them somehow,' cried the merchant. 'Can we swim over to it?'

'We must, master,' his servant replied, 'or die in the attempt.'

Summoning their remaining strength, the men struggled over to the stern of the mysterious ship. Ropes were hanging down and they managed to haul themselves on to its deck. There they each collapsed into a sleep full of strange dreams. When they eventually awoke it seemed as if their dreams were continuing. All around them were skeletons dressed in old fashioned sailors' clothing. One was tied to the main mast and was wearing what had once been a fine coat. It had a red scarf around its skeleton neck and a sword hung from the broad belt buckled round its waist.

'Master,' said the servant quietly, 'this seems to be a ship of the dead.'

'At least she seems seaworthy and she has a good compass so we can direct her to Tangiers. I think I'd like to get rid of the skeletons though.'

The two men tried to push the skeletons overboard but they wouldn't be moved. It was as though they had become part of the boat.

food and some very old fashioned clothing. It was good to have dry clothes and a full stomach. Then they were so tired that they each found a clean bunk and fell asleep once more.

Suddenly, there was a loud crash and the ship gave a lurch which woke them up. On deck they saw that the ropes holding the wheel had snapped and they were drifting aimlessly. Once again, they needed all their strength to get the ship back on course. From then on one of them always stayed by the wheel in case the ropes should break again.

'I'm afraid they're going to remain our companions for the voyage,' said the merchant. 'We'll just have to make the most of it.'

He went to the big ship's wheel and tried to change course to head for Tangiers, but he couldn't shift it.

'Come and help!' he shouted to his servant.

It was all they could do to turn the wheel between them, but somehow they managed and the strange ship began its voyage to Tangiers.

Once the men had set course they bound the wheel with strong rope and explored the boat. They found

After a long, exhausting journey, the two men arrived at Tangiers and dropped anchor in the harbour.

'Master,' said the servant, 'I know someone who might be able to find out the truth about this boat.'

The merchant was slumped in a corner of the deck. 'I'm so exhausted I can hardly move. You fetch your friend and I'll rest for a while.'

The servant returned an hour or so later with a tall man dressed in a dark cloak which he pulled all around him so that you could scarcely see his face.

This man had a leather bag full of earth which he had baked dry in a fire.

He went to each of the skeletons in turn and sprinkled a little of the dust, first on the hands and then on the feet. As the dust touched the hands, the bones became men again but as soon as it touched the feet they melted away.

Tired though he was, the rich merchant sprang to his feet. 'Who are you?' he asked the man in black. 'What are you doing?' Without answering him, the man went to the skeleton tied to the mast and dusted just the hands. The bones became a fine figure of a man with bright eyes, a flashing smile and a neat black beard. The ropes holding him fell away and he stood before them and spoke.

'At last!' he said. 'I thought nobody would ever save us. Now I must tell you our sad story. Long ago, when we were young, we sailed the seas carrying whatever cargo we could. Once we gave passage to a strange man with a bag that he would let nobody else touch. We thought it must be treasure and I am ashamed to say that we seized him and bundled him over the side. As he hit the sea he put a curse on us ... that we would never find peace until our feet and hands touched dry land. We were young and nothing scared us. We rushed to his cabin but all the bag had in it was dried herbs. There was no treasure then, but lots later. The curse was on us and whenever we tried to put into harbour the boat wouldn't go where we wanted. So we hoisted the black flag and became pirates. We boarded many ships and stole from each of them, though somehow we managed to avoid killing anyone. All that was long ago. Time went by and one by one we became the skeletons you found. I tied myself to the mast hoping that some day somebody would help us. Today, my friends, you have indeed broken the curse. I offer my heartfelt thanks to you.'

When he had finished speaking, the man sprinkled the last of the dry earth on to his feet and he too faded away.

So my story goes and so it ends.